CLIMBING THE WRITING WALL

Dana Gerow

Tadhg Gerow

Cover design by Falcon Giraux

Western World Tree Press

www.westernworldtreepress.com

Climbing the Writing Wall

Copyright @ 2015 by

Dana Gerow and

Tadhg Gerow

ISBN-13: 978-1493558704

ISBN-10: 1493558706

A Western World Tree Press Book

www.westernworldtreepress.com

Printed in the United States of America

0 9 8 7 6 5 4 3 2 1

Table of Contents

Climbing the Writing Wall

What is the message?

About 30 years ago, I took a play writing course. It was a time when students would go to dinner with their professors or meet outside of class for a drink. The educational climate has changed a lot. Education seems to have devolved from the creation of relationships and the exploration of ideas to one of the absorption of knowledge for its sake alone without consideration for how this knowledge fits into the matrix of the individual. Perhaps as we become more social via all of our social networking media, we are actually becoming less social, i.e. creating more social interactions, but less meaningful social interactions.

That is a topic of debate for another day. I simply wanted to set the scene and time period.

Anna, my play writing professor, and I sat down for coffee. I explained the plot of the play, that the story line was really about a number of people's lives intersecting in one place. She asked me what the message of the play was. I told her that I thought the message might be random, that life is absolute chaos.

She replied, "Not good enough."

I said, "Why?"

She said, "In your journal or your diary, life can be random or chaotic, but on the stage, as an art form, life is distilled presence. There is a meaning behind what happens, a message that is meant for the audience-- communicated through dialogue and story."

I said, "But life is chaotic. What is the meaning of a cup of coffee, or a sunny day, or a tragedy. Stuff happens. Keep moving. Get over it."

She replied. "Is that your message?"

"Get over it? Maybe? Why does a play need to have a message? Why not just present everything and let the viewers make sense of it in their own way? Everyone is going to make sense of it in their own way anyway?"

She answered, "Because writing is communicating. Even if you wanted to represent chaos, it would be coming through your filter, your eyes. You will, whether you wish to or not, create a landscape of the soul and a message of the mind. You can't help it. What I am telling you is that as an artist-- you need to be conscious of that message."

"What if there is no message?"

"Then, you need to ask yourself if there is communication happening between the writer and the reader. What is the writer's reason to write? What is the reader's reason to read it?"

That day stuck with me. With the arrogance of youth, it still took me some months to actually process what Anna was trying to convey to me. And then, I started to see meaning in all sorts of acts that I had otherwise taken for granted. Graffiti on the wall in the subway was not just random. It was put there by someone in the hopes that it would be seen, that it would convey some message to the world. Logos and billboards, architecture and design all were creations that were meant to convey some concept to the viewer. Writing, film, theater, art and dance were all media for a message, filtered through the eyes of the creator. We engage in these media because the media becomes something like a conversation between the creator and the "createe". Even anthropologists spend hours at digs of ancient sites in the hopes that the relics of an ancient time still have a message for people today?

One of my first lessons was the need to be conscious that communication is meant for an audience--ideally. What is the message?

Planning the journey

In a thousand high school classrooms around the world, some English teacher somewhere is teaching "thesis statement". I used to think this was a kind of purgatory assigned to the beleaguered teacher for some past life sin and assigned to us as students as a punishment for original sin. To be honest, if the idea could be summed up in one sentence, why not do that and get on with life? If the ideas needed to be experience to be understood, then how on earth could one sum up the idea in just one sentence?

The ultimate paradox.

It was not until I was much older that I truly understood that writing is a journey. The journey is not just about the destination. If it were, I could say, "Buffalo. There, you have it. That's the essay." But what does this communicate to someone who has never been to Buffalo? The reader is signing up for the journey.

If writing is a journey, then a thesis statement is a Triptik or travel itinerary. The thesis might tell you where you want to go, but it also tells you how you are going to see it. What famous sites will you visit? Is there a "theme" to this trip such as famous architecture, famous landmarks, regional food? Therefore, a thesis statement is not the journey, but a plan for the journey.

I like to use a little mnemonic to help me with creating thesis statements.

First you need to know your destination, i.e. topic.

Then, you need to know how you will explore this place, i.e. a theme.

Last, you need your itinerary, i.e. places you will visit.

For example, my triptik might look like this

We will visit the fine city of Buffalo with an eye toward exploring the following parks designed by Fredrick Law Olmsted: Cazenovia Park, Front Park, and Delaware Park.

If you were reading this statement as a potential traveler, you would know where you were going, how you were going to explore this place and some of the points of interest. This is basically the purpose of a thesis statement. It is not the journey. It is the itinerary, and the itinerary is as important for the writer to know as it is for the reader to know. The writer may be the tour guide and the reader may be the tourist, but the truth is that this journey is going to be taken together. The best laid plans may go astray, but there are still plenty of reasons why making a plan is better than not making a plan.

Think about your own city. If you were going to explore your city, how would you do this? What sites would you visit? Create your own triptik. Now, you are one step closer to understanding a thesis statement.

Building the idea bank

When I was first studying the teaching of writing, one of the first exercises Dr. James Collins asked us to do was to "free write". Free writing involves putting pen to paper and letting thought and ink spill down the page in a random, free-form style. At the end of ten minutes, he asked us to put our pens down and read through what we had written. I looked at my paper. It was a mess of conflicting thoughts, ideas, memories, etc. This is what a lot of students think writing is... physically the act of writing.

We tried another form of brainstorming, clustering. This is the act of putting a central thematic idea on the page, such as "Great Travel Destinations" and drawing bubbles off the main theme with locales like Cancun, Maine, Chicago, New Orleans, Paris, Shanghai, Berlin, New York City and London. You can draw bubbles off of these bubbles and add places like the Eiffel Tower, Times Square, Piccadilly Circus, etc. These might eventually make great travelogues for those cities. In any case, this exercise can rapidly help the writer to create his or her bucket list.

The question is whether free writing and clustering are actually communication.

Free writing is stream of consciousness, something like a dream. I think this is why dreams are so difficult to remember in the morning. An apple appears beside a teddy bear beside a train wreck and someone calling to their dog.... The process of sorting dreams is something akin to finding meaning in studying tea leaves at the bottom of one's cup to find a message. The message is going to be highly dependent upon the person interpreting these tea leaves. The act itself is like looking for shapes in the clouds or listening to the words of the Oracle at Delphi. What one notices in the message is what is important to oneself. And this will be different for every person who approaches this chaos of words. However. there can by nuggets of pure gold amid the sand and debris. Sometimes, the writer needs to sift through by circling ideas that stand out in order to build an idea bank.

Clustering can be a bit more formulaic in terms of its process and its results. The main bubble can be divided into subsets. Ideally, the bubbles share some common thematic relationships. Clustering can spark ideas. I have used this technique more than once in community think tanks to quickly appraise levels of interest for various topics in the room. Clustering can serve as a warehouse of ideas, but in order to go into any depth, ultimately, one has to pick an idea to focus on.

The better question is whether free writing and clustering are effective forms of communication. I think that these and other brainstorming exercises can be interesting ways for the writer to explore his or her own thoughts and feelings. These activities, both individually and in group think tanks, can produce great idea lists, places to start wonderful discussions, debates, even research concepts.

Here's the rub though. Ideas are only ideas, however, until you do something more with them.

The physical act of writing

Timed Writing-- every student dreads it.

At one point in my career, that was my job. I walked into a room full of students who had failed the standardized timed writing tests and taught them how to pass these kinds of exams. The class had all the enthusiasm of prisoners doing time, and liked me about as much as they would like the jailer. I had my work cut out for me.

Invariably, I would begin the course with an object lesson. I would put a writing prompt on the screen. I have collected hundreds of these prompts over the years, but let's say that I was using this prompt, "Schools are considering extended year programming. This would mean a reduced summer vacation. Tell me why this is a good idea, or why this is not a good idea. You have 45 minutes to convince me in essay format." The topic was a good one for a room full of students who were missing out on their summer vacation because of a failed exam. More than a few glares were launched in my direction.

I hit the timer.

Pens flew. Ink ran. It was like watching a flock of gazelle fleeing before the proverbial lion. Words scrawled across the pages. The timer counted down the minutes. And then, something strange happened. One by one at about 20 minutes into the exercise, students would raise their hands, push a mass of papers in my direction and then dejectedly put their heads down on the desk. I would ask, "Are you sure that you don't need more time? Do you want to rewrite this?"

The student would roll her eyes. "Why would I want more time? I hate this question. The essay sucks."

And so, I would gather the papers and wait until the last person had finished the test. Then, I would hand all the papers back and tell them, "This is not writing. This is free writing. There is a key difference between physically writing and actually writing. The difference is planning."

Why I hate outlines

My high school English teacher was a Canadian lady of indeterminate age, but it had to be over 100. Her hair was gray. She wore gray. Her name was Miss Gray, and we studied from dog-eared textbooks that were so old that they might as well have been gray. Roll the introductory scenes of "A Christmas Carol" where Ebenezer Scrooge sits hunched over a desk with his head bowed in defeat as he writes out arcane punctuation rules for the 50th time.

That was my childhood. Heaven only knows why I became a writing teacher. Perhaps it was so that I could prove to myself that teaching writing need not be like walking into the maw of hell and marching straight through the last circles of Dante's Inferno-- or worse, personally living out the story of a character out of a Charles Dickens' novel.

One of the exercises that we did until tears ran from my eyes was the art of outlining. I can still hear Mrs. Gray saying that there is a main topic and then subtopics which are marked in Roman numerals and then ideas for developing each subtopic which are marked either in capital letters or lower case letters depending upon whether they are main ideas or minor ideas. I could outline in my sleep, and I also thought that the whole exercise was useless.

While I crave organization as much as the next person, I also think that there may be a point at which organization for organization's sake might be like counting peas as they go into the pot or lining up the tater tots into neat little rows as they go onto the baking sheet. Is the effort worth the reward? Is this important enough to spend time on? While there may be projects that are so detailed that they would benefit from a formal outline, I think that it may be a mistake to outline shorter pieces of writing with more immediate currency.

Instead, I like this approach. I tell the students to think about their topic and to consider their audience. What are the questions that your readers will have about your topic? This can also work as a great collaboration exercise. The writer explains to the group what it is that he or she is writing about and what angle he or she will take with the piece. For example, the writer may be approaching the task of writing about Buffalo by looking at the various Olmsted parks. From here, the group can brainstorm questions that they might have.

1. Who is Fredrick Law Olmsted?

2. Why is he well-known for developing city parks?

3. What cities did he work with?

4. Why was Buffalo one of those cities?

5. What is unique about Cazenovia Park?

6. What is unique about Front Park?

7. What is unique about Delaware Park?

Collaboration can be so cool! It is amazing what a group of minds can come up with. I like this sort of exercise because in the process of creating these questions, the writer really gets a sense that there is an audience, that communication is an interactive process. The readers want to learn about a topic, and it is the writer's job to explain, explore, even teach. As readers, we do come to the art of reading with certain expectations. We want to understand. We want to learn. We want to come away from the experience with more ideas than we had before. It is the writer's job to communicate these ideas in the clearest manner possible. It is fair to play both roles in this exercise. Good chess players are always thinking about their own moves and guessing the moves of the other player as well. Good communication involves this sort of exchange.

What questions would your readers ask about your triptik through your travel destination?

Why ask a question?

At the end of another community college class, I
was packing up all my books, papers and supplies
into my cavernous backpack. I was working as a
professor in a rural college. It was an odd
experience. I was at the front of the class with chalk
and a blackboard. They were in their seats with
their notebooks open. I wanted so much to step
inside their worlds and to help them to express the
ideas that were percolating there. On certain days,
that divide felt like The Grand Canyon. I felt as if
perhaps I was preaching from the mountaintop and
hoping that they could hear me in the valley, or as if
I were standing at the edge of the woods shouting to
people lost in the woods about how nice it was out
here in the sunshine. From looking at their faces,
or even pausing to ask meaningful questions, I
realized that I had no idea if I was getting through,
or if anything I was saying was making the least bit
of sense to them. Indeed, I was beginning to
wonder if lecturing was even the best method of
teaching?

It was on such a day as I was putting away my
staplers, dictionary, thesaurus, white-out, extra pens
and paper, et cetera that one of my students stayed
after for extra help. My heavens, how computers
have simplified our lives. I can't imagine how I
carried 50 pounds of supplies from room to room

in the college. We truly are blessed by new technology.

He was a mountain of a man, blonde with untidy hair, and a permanent sunburn that I had come to associate with many of my students who came from the neighboring farms to take classes.

"My assignment is not done," he said.

"Is everything okay?" I asked.

Larry shrugged. "I guess I have nothing to say."

At this point, I motioned for him to pull up two chairs. "Larry, of course, you have something to say. Write about anything. What about your friends, hobbies?"

Larry shrugged. The longer he sat there, the more vague his eyes became. "I have friends. They don't do anything special."

"Hobbies?"

"We mostly go shooting deer. You don't talk much when you're hunting."

"Family?" I asked.

I knew I had hit a sore subject. Larry winced. "In case, you didn't notice, I'm slow. When they start talking, I can't keep up. By the time I come up with something to share, they are onto the next thing. Anymore, I just listen."

"Then, you must know a lot," I said. "Because the people who listen end up knowing twice as much as the people who talk."

Larry smiled. "I must know a lot. I have 14 brothers and sisters. I can't get a word in edgewise."

"You just need to ask yourself the right questions, questions that make you really think about the issue. You might not answer the question immediately. That's okay. That's the wonderful thing about writing. The paper is very patient. It will wait as you put together your thoughts."

We started listing Larry's questions about NASA. It turned out that this young man had a budding interest in exploring in space exploration. Who knew? He was slow to speak, but with pen in hand, he had found his voice.

Do you ever struggle with finding your voice? Are there situations in which you have so much to say that you find yourself saying nothing at all? If you were trying to get your thoughts onto paper, what questions would you ask yourself?

Paragraph Jeopardy

I used to play a game that I called "Paragraph Jeopardy" with my community college students. I would cut out paragraphs from a variety of magazines and put them in a hat. The student had to pick a paragraph out of the hat and read the paragraph out loud. Then, we all tried to figure out what question the paragraph was answering. It might seem tediously pointless, but it's not. A well-written article is like a running engine. It works. You can simply sit back and admire the form and the smooth prose. It's an art form. However, if you want to become a writer, you need to do more than admire good writers. You need to analyze what a good writer is doing and why the process works.

If you want to take apart what the writer intended, just look at each paragraph and ask yourself, "What question was the writer trying to answer here?" Pretty soon, you will have a list of questions similar to our triptik in the previous exercise. You can even list the answers that the writer used to answer each of his or her questions. This is an interesting exercise to try out with a wide variety of articles, such as science, history, finance, and the arts. Dollars to donuts, those articles which seemed very clear and well-structured had questions that you could easily intuit.

There is something to be learned from unclear or vague writing as well. One of the first things that you will notice as you try to reverse engineer what the writer did is that the questions will be difficult to figure out. The writer may even have numerous questions locked inside a single paragraph or may start out with one question, drop it, and answer another, perhaps unrelated, question. If the feeling the writer is going for is an artistic stream of consciousness, well then, this will do it. If the prose are supposed to be like poetry in which every reader logs in a different experience, then, go for it. It is useful to read something that is purposefully vague or recursive in order to understand that while such writing may create an "experience", it is not especially effective at communicating or educating others.

For the most part, students who are coming into writing courses are doing so because they wish to write to be understood. Their jobs may require them to write technical support materials or detailed medical reports or even instructions for others to follow. In this sort of writing, it is not a plus if your readers all come away from the piece with a different experience. It is best if your reader can intuit which questions you were answering, if you spend a sufficient amount of energy and information in answering each question and if you transition to a new paragraph when you stop answering one question and start answering another.

For this reason, it is good to "deconstruct" another writer's piece to get down to those basic questions, to see how the writer answered those questions, and to try to determine why the writer put the questions in the order that he or she did. This is an excellent exercise to prepare you for setting up your own informal outline.

What articles did you read this week? Could you figure out which questions the author was answering?

How to answer the question

This is a question that often comes up when students are working with question and answer technique. The question serves as a great way to start. A lot of brainstorming ideas come to the fore. Then, it's time to write. Writing means organizing. It's the difference between digging for gems and cutting and polishing those gems.

Let's look at an example.

Why are companies leveraging employees who work from home?

1. It's often cheaper to keep a smaller physical office space.

2. Telecommuting to a Sharepoint site is as productive as working in the office.

3. More business is being done online.

4. Buyers often visit the website first.

5. Employee is responsible for his or her own computer/office equipment.

6. Live teleconferencing is almost as good as meeting in person.

7. Employees can spend more time actually working instead of commuting.

8. Work from home agreements allow employers to hire people who may be highly qualified, but are not local.

9. Employer may hire the employee on as a "consultant" and thus pay for a job done as opposed to hourly wage, which may be financially a good approach for the company.

After you brainstorm your answers, you may find that some of the answers don't "fit" in the paragraph. This may be because they are actually answering other questions. If you look at our example above, which answers seem as if they might actually belong in a separate paragraph?

If you picked #3 and #4, you are learning to sift answers that belong from those that do not. Actually, those two answers have more to do with why companies are shifting their focus to online presence and sales. This might feed into the need/desire to hire employees who work from home, but this question probably deserves its own paragraph, perhaps before this paragraph.

Now, how do you turn this brainstorming into a paragraph?

The easy way to look at the question is that if you turn the question into a statement, it can become a topic sentence. Topic sentences, as we learned in our grammar school days, go at the beginning of the paragraph.

Question: Why are companies leveraging employees who work from home?

Statement: Employers are increasingly leveraging employees who work from home for a number of good reasons.

Now, sort your answers in a way that makes sense. You might want more general answers to go first and then move to more specific answers as you develop the paragraph or you might sort by areas of interest.

Employers often choose work-from-home agreements with employees for financial reasons. First, it's often cheaper to keep a smaller physical office space. In addition, the employee is responsible for his or her own computer/office equipment. Productivity is another factor. Employees can spend more time actually working instead of commuting. Also, an employer may hire the employee on as a "consultant" and thus pay for a job done as opposed to hourly wage. This puts the onus of responsibility for meeting deadlines on the consultant who agrees to the contract. Moreover, technology is making it much easier for companies to work in new ways. Telecommuting to a sharepoint site is as productive as working in the office. Live teleconferencing is almost as good as meeting in person. Lastly, there is the issue of employee qualifications. Work from home agreements allow employers to hire people who may be highly qualified, but are not local.

Your last sentence of your paragraph might sum up the main points or lead into your next paragraph.

Summary: Thus, the growing trend of employers setting up work-from-home agreements with employees may have some very sound reasons.

Let's put it all together, shall we?

Sample Paragraph:

Employers are increasingly leveraging employees who work from home for a number of good reasons. Frequently, employers choose work-from-home agreements with employees for financial reasons. First, it's often cheaper to keep a smaller physical office space. In addition, the employee is responsible for his or her own computer/office equipment. Productivity is another factor. Employees can spend more time actually working instead of commuting. Also, an employer may hire the employee on as a "consultant" and thus pay for a job done as opposed to hourly wage. This puts the onus of responsibility for meeting deadlines on the consultant who agrees to the contract. Moreover, technology is making it much easier for companies to work in new ways. Telecommuting to a sharepoint site is as productive as working in the office. Live teleconferencing is almost as good as meeting in person. Lastly, there is the issue of employee qualifications. Work from home agreements allow employers to hire people who may be highly qualified, but are not local. Thus, the growing trend of employers setting up work-from-home agreements with employees may have some very sound reasons.

This method of breaking down writing into its pieces and parts may seem a little tedious at first. However, what this method lacks in artistry, it gains back in clarity. As I always say, "Be clear about what you are trying to communicate first and foremost. Style and artistry can come later."

Try this out with the question that we did not work with. Why are businesses becoming more concerned with their online presence? What are the first steps you will take as you figure out how to develop a paragraph to answer this question?

Asking the right questions

In any conversation, there are turns of phrases which are deal breakers. Most of these deal breakers come in the form of ultimatums. You've probably seen the exchange between husbands and wives. The conversation turns heated, and suddenly, the exchanges become about fixing the other person. The husband puts his hands on his hips and says, "Do you or don't you want to take a vacation this year?" This is not as extreme as an ultimatum, but it is next door to it. This is a closed question, and the effect of a closed question is that it really closes off further communication. In the case of the scenario above, there really are only two ways to answer this question: yes or no. I suppose you could get by with a maybe, but that is not what the question is asking for.

Therefore, if the purpose of the question is to keep the conversation going, to keep exploring the topic, then one would need to avoid closed questions and try to offer up many open-ended questions. Open-ended questions don't seek a yes or no answer, but rather to explore all the possibilities. An open-ended question might be "Where would you like to go on vacation this year?" or "How would you like to travel?". These types of questions open up the conversation to explore potential answers. As a small piece of marriage advice, it is probably better to engage with an open-ended question as opposed to a closed question. You might not always get all the answers that you want, but you will keep the dialogue going, which is rather important in a long term relationship.

In terms of writing, the idea is to explore the topic. Closed questions are artificially easy. Certainly, you can ask a question such as "Are trade agreements good for the US or not?" Certainly, you could answer yes or no to this question; however, there is a lot that is not explored in a simple yes or no response, such as why. "Why does the US engage in trade agreements?" "What does the US hope to gain by initiating a trade agreement?" These might be questions that would be not be covered by a simple yes or no. I imagine an entire book of exploration could be dedicated to the exploration of these sorts of topics. Therefore, although the impatience of human nature wants a definitive response, a definite "yes" or "no", don't be lulled into walking down that merry path, for therein lies the road to ignorance.

Instead, choose open-ended questions. These might start out as "how", "what", "why", etc. The key to whether your questions are open-ended or not is that open-ended questions will not be easy to answer. One word or even one sentence will not suffice to put the question to rest. When you find yourself naturally developing these kinds of questions, you are one step closer to becoming a writer.

Dipping your tea cup into the ocean AKA research

Part of the joy of writing is finding out something that you did not know before. If you always knew what the answer would be, how much fun would it be to ask? This goes back to that old saying that the more I learn, the less I know. Sadly and wonderfully as well, this is the end result of learning. Oh to be as young and certain of all things as I was when I was a child...

By now, you have probably begun to think about topics and questions that beg you to answer them. You could probably devise questions that could fuel your own research study. That would be a topic for an entirely different conversation. However, most of the time, one would begin one's exploration by researching what others have done before you. To paraphrase Isaac Newton, we can see as far and as well as we do because we stand on the shoulders of giants. We might want to improve upon the wheel, but there is no need to recreate the wheel. Therefore, we need to know where other researchers have gone before.

We also need to make sure that our topic is "researchable". There are two ways in which a topic can be non-researchable. First, the idea could be so new that people have not yet done any research on it. At the time of this writing, gay marriage has just been legalized in the US. Therefore, at the time of this writing, one would expect that there might not be too much in the way of research on gay divorce yet. The other way in which a topic can be non-researchable is when it is so broad, and so many people have written on it, that sifting through the articles that come back from a search might be akin to looking for a needle in a haystack. A topic such as abortion or the death penalty has received so much press on either side of the aisle that it has become very difficult to research actually. The number of opinion articles actually displaces any legitimate research. Both of these extremes present problems when one is trying to research.

The solution is to choose an interesting angle. You can choose a topic that has been opined to meaninglessness if you choose an angle that cuts down on the number of articles you will bring up in your library search. For example, the word "abortion" may bring up close to a million articles. This is not going to be helpful as one would have to sift through a million titles. However, if one narrows the search with the boolean "AND", the number of articles can become focused very rapidly. For example, "abortion" AND "infertility treatment" actually might only give 5,000 articles. This becomes much easier to scan through. If one needed to narrow the number of articles still, one could search by adding another search term.

When I was in graduate school, libraries were just transitioning from the old card catalog system to electronic searches using key terms. There were still stacks of magazines on the shelves and aisles and aisles of books and microfiche. Walking into the library was still a little like walking into a church--very quiet and full of old things. The computers actually looked like they really did not belong there at all and were relegated to one small corner away from all the real library work.

I remember quite well my first internet search. I was looking up the word "antibiotic". The search came back with 10,000 articles. I was at a loss. My hands became sweaty. I started at the screen in depressed horror. How could I read 10,000 articles? It would certainly take me weeks to do so. My paper was due next week. I read until I fell asleep at the terminal and had to be shaken awake by a testy librarian. Immediately, I visited my professor's office hours to complain against this injustice. My professor kindly explained that the difference between an effective library search and an ineffective library search was in the use of "key terms". No, I was not expected to read 10,000 articles.

Yes, it is possible to reach information overload very rapidly when one is searching in electronic databases, e-libraries or on the internet. Be mindful of the signs. If your search is bringing back so many articles that you are unable to scan the titles and sort the ones that might be useful, then you have come down with this dreaded illness, information overload. The cure is to come up with more exact search terms for the information that you want.

Have you ever felt while doing research as if you were trying to gather an ocean of information into a teacup? How did you narrow your search to get past the information overload?

Key terms versus information overload

Some topics are naturally narrow enough. The field is so small or so new or so niche that there may not be a lot written about it. In these cases, the battle may be to find enough information without necessarily compromising your standards, i.e. some information sources are more reliable than others.

However, if the topic has been discussed for any length of time, a growing amount of research, data, analysis and opinion is going to grow up all around it like weeds choking out your prize roses. When this happens, a single word or idea often will not be enough to limit the information search and weed out what you don't want from what you do want. In this case, you might need more key terms in order to sift through the mountain of information. Don't just assume that as you sit looking at the library screen that magic will happen and that you will amazingly come up with great key terms on the spot. The truth is that under the gun, you are more likely to become frustrated than to become amazing. Therefore, it is best to plan out your list of key terms in advance.

This is where guided freewriting can be a boon. At the top of the paper or blank Word document, however you like to draft, write out these questions: "Why does this topic really interest me? What new perspectives do I want to bring to this discussion?"

Then, set your timer. Some people swear by five minutes. Others swear by 10 or 15 minutes. It's up to you. Don't give up if it is slow going as you start. If you really start coming up with a lot of ideas, ignore the timer. Just write until you capture it all.

When you are finished, you may want to put your freewriting away for a bit. I know when I have just finished writing something, I am still excited about having created the piece. It takes a little while for me to be able to come back to it and analyze the work. You may need an hour, a few hours or even a day. When you come back to it, you will want to be looking for key phrases that describe exactly what you are looking for. These do not need to be single words. Phrases such as "nonprofit daycare centers" will work also. Just remember that your search engine may require you to put word strings in quotation marks to make sure that the system searches for that string of words as a phrase instead of those individual words anywhere at all in the article. Write down your list of key terms before you search in the library so that if your first search doesn't yield promising results, you can always try another combination of key terms.

Some people are just naturally gifted. Key terms come to them easily. They may also cheat and use a thesaurus or synonym finder in order to come up with related terms. If you are truly one of those amazing people, don't let me stop you. Start your search. If you are not one of those amazing people, don't worry. With enough practice, you will become one.

What strategies did you try in order to come up with key terms for your topic? Why do you think these key terms will limit the playing field and provide you with the information you seek?

Analyzing the value of online data

Libraries used to be the repositories of all knowledge. Yes, some of us still cry over the burning of the Library of Alexandria. Imagine what could have been saved if they had had the internet in Julius Caesar's day!

Now, it might be just as easy to sit in your living room with a cup of cocoa and your laptop on the coffee table and peruse the internet for the information you seek.

However, it should be noted that not all online information sites are created equal. Some are just plain better than others. Still, the first site that most people will visit will be Wikipedia. It's not always a bad instinct as long as you approach this task correctly.

First off, Wikipedia is "user-generated". This means that Wikipedia doesn't necessarily have a staff of editors who are reading all the articles and checking for accuracy. Wikipedia is usually much, much better as a resource than a discussion board, blog, or chat room.

However, here is the reason why.

Wikipedia may be user-generated, but this does not mean that these users are uninformed. Indeed, frequently, these "users" may be university professors who are just doing their part to provide accurate information to the masses.

One of the ways that you can tell whether or not the writer was well-informed would be to scan to the bottom of the article and look at the writer's references page. These articles should be published in established magazines and journals with an editorial staff checking for accuracy.

You may want to print out these references and then plug these author's names and article titles into an e-library. If you are in college, you probably have access to an e-library with digital articles and books. If you are not enrolled in a college at present, you may want to use your local library or check out Google Scholar: https://scholar.google.com/.

If you are researching a medical question, you may want to access the national databank of medically related articles:

http://www.ncbi.nlm.nih.gov/pubmed.

Both of these search engines should provide peer-referenced articles.

With regard to openly searching the internet on Google, Yahoo, or Bing, you get what you pay for— so to speak. These search engines are paid for by advertising, so don't be too surprised when you find that their advertisers' links come up first.

Just because someone pays to advertise does not necessarily make that website the premiere expert on the topic.

Be cautious.

Sometimes, when I want to cut through the extraneous results, I go to a smaller search engine that doesn't save search information. That search engine is https://duckduckgo.com/.

Have you visited Wikipedia and looked up the reference articles you found there? Did this help you to get started on your research journey? Have you visited the public databases that are available to you? How did this help you in terms of your research process?

The value of a website

More and more, people are turning to the internet to find information. As mentioned before, not everything that is written is true. Not everything that you find on the internet is credible. Regardless of what search engine you decide to use, you need to look for four things once you get there:

1. How current is this information?
2. Is this website trying to sell me a product?
3. Do the authors list their references? Is this information corroborated anywhere else?
4. What type of website is this? Is this a dot gov, dot org, dot edu, dot net or dot com website?

Back in the day when it was the coolest thing to claim a domain name and to create your own personal website, people jumped on the bandwagon and grabbed domain names and set up websites. Often, these would be filled with personal blogs or opinion pieces. The internet was very young. Internet visitors have since become much more savvy. However, this is one of the reasons why it is important to check the last update of the website. Frequently, you can find this information at the top or bottom of the article that you are looking at. Sometimes, you will see a copyright date. If you cannot find the date listed with the article, go back to the home page for the website and look to see when the website was last updated. The year is important. If the date in question is more than five years old, the information you are looking at might not be the most current information you can find.

The second criterion is probably the easiest. As you are looking through the website, do you find that the website is selling a product? If so, you need to ask yourself whether the information you are looking at is skewed to sell that product?

Why would people do that? Profit, of course.

If you find that the website is selling a product, you may wish to take everything you read with a grain of salt. Some of the information presented there might be true, but remember that the primary goal of that information is to persuade you to buy that product. This might not be your best resource. If the website presents references, then you may wish to fact-check any information you find.

Products are not the only things that a website can sell. Sometimes, a website is created to sell a point of view or a political agenda. A thoughtful, well-written article will be careful not to use "inflammatory" language. This means that if the author is really seeking to disseminate information, he or she will do just that. They will give you information, and let you decide how you feel about it. If the article uses language that is supposed to make you feel sad, sorry, angry, upset or scared, then the primary purpose of the article is NOT to disseminate information. The primary purpose of the article is to get you to support an idea or agenda. Be careful. Use your "BS" detector. Recognize when someone is trying to manipulate you with something other than impartial information. Another key word you may find in these types of sites is "The Truth". Think about that for a moment.

There is an old story about the blindfolded people who are asked to identify an animal based on what they feel. One has the leg and says it is a tree. One has the tail and says it is a snake. So the story goes. The animal is an elephant, of course. "The Truth" is a little like this. Based on a person's perceptions, the truth can be different things to different people. Be careful when you read about other people's truths. These truths are based on their perceptions and life experiences. Be careful when you present your own "truth" as your "truth" is based upon your own perceptions and life experiences.

Lastly, look at the website itself. The website address may indicate the type of organization which created the website. The government is allowed to use dot gov website addresses. Educational organizations are allowed to use dot edu website addresses. Organizations are allowed to use dot org website addresses. Private parties may use dot net or dot com addresses. In general, government and educational resources have probably been fact-checked. Organizational information may very well have been fact-checked. Information from private parties, including businesses, may or may not have been fact-checked.

The cardinal rule is this.

Always check your sources!

Order out of chaos

When one has all one's information together and some plan for questions one is going to answer, the common consensus is to put all the information in some order that is going to make sense to the reader. This is more challenging than we give this process credit for. Obviously, different people think differently, and they come to any learning experience with different levels of prior knowledge. A woman who has been working on cars all her life is going to come at the challenge of learning a new electrical system in a much different way from someone who has never worked on a car ever. Prior knowledge is a challenge because the writer would obviously want to make the piece interesting for all audiences-- and understandable for all audiences as well.

What makes sense is not necessarily as easy to figure out as it might seem to be.

One way to look at how to put information into an understandable order is to consider "patterns". The human mind is interesting in this fashion. We tend to see patterns in things. We also tend to create in patterns. Some people think this is why older drivers have faster reflexes than younger drivers. Older drivers see patterns in traffic. Some patterns spell trouble. The more experienced drivers are faster at assessing this and making defensive choices because they have seen these patterns before. Younger drivers actually physically don't have slower reflex time, but rather take longer to assess a situation because they don't have these experiential patterns to draw from.

This is why I suggested in a previous chapter to analyze the work of other authors. Look carefully at the questions their paragraphs are answering. Then, line the questions up. Is there a pattern to how the piece is organized? Many experienced writers create patterns without even realizing that they are using a pattern. However, you can learn to write in new ways by closely examining the patterns that these writers create.

Obviously, most pieces have an opening and a conclusion. We see this pattern a lot. There are often prologues and epilogues in books. In the theater, the curtain opens when the play begins and closes when the play ends. The audience is expected to clap. Even television shows have opening scenes which show relevant pieces of the story from the prior episode and end with teaser scenes from the upcoming episode. This is a pattern that we are very familiar with. Rarely, do we expect the reader to jump into the middle of the story and simply try to make sense of it. However, there are many other patterns at play in writing.

In your analysis of other writers' articles, what patterns are you seeing? You can learn a lot about how to be a better writer by simply reading and analyzing what you are reading. My suggestion for this exercise might be to simply read the paragraph for fun first. Enjoy. Reflect on how you felt about the topic when you started the article and how you felt about the topic when you finished the article.

Next, go through the article. Look at the introductory paragraph. How did the writer get you interested in this topic? What did the author promise as you started reading the piece?

Then, look at the conclusion. How did the author close this piece? How did the closing impact how you feel about the topic? Did the closing answer the questions that were raised in the opening?

Finally, look at each paragraph and ask what question the paragraph was answering. If you list out these questions as the writer addressed them in the article, do they create a pattern? How would you describe this pattern?

Be Original!

I am going to take a page out of the parenting books and say that negative commands are not as powerful as positive commands. Therefore, the lecture on "Don't plagiarize!" should in my opinion be changed to "Be original!". The reason for this is clear. Telling people not to do something does not actually tell them what to do instead. Right? Do you catch my drift here? While I think it is important to tell people what plagiarism is and why it is important to avoid it, I think it is equally important to tell people what work practices to implement instead.

Therefore, let's talk about what plagiarism is. Plagiarism is actively or passively presenting someone else's work as your own. However, you can say that there is nothing new under the sun. How is it possible to have an original thought that someone else has not thought of before. The truth is that the old saying is actually wrong. A million snowflakes fall and yet each one is a unique, one-of-a-kind design. New inventions are being created daily that never existed before this moment, and new research is being done that is adding to our knowledge of the universe on a daily basis. This period in time is not called the information age for nothing. Likewise, your essay on global economy will be like no other essay on global economy unless, of course, you actually copy and paste someone else's words onto your page and try to pass it off as your work. That is plagiarism in its most overt and active form. There is, however, also a passive form of plagiarism, which is using someone else's data, research findings or theories and presenting these as your own by means of not citing your sources. This is a little less overt, but is plagiarism nonetheless.

As Isaac Newton suggested, we see as far as we do because stand on the shoulders of giants. Therefore, no one expects you to recreate the wheel, only to give credit where credit is due. This is more a matter of study habits, i.e. carefully reading and taking notes. When you are reading an article or book or website and you come across interesting information, it is important to do two things.

1. Write down the interesting fact, statistic, data, theory or findings in your notes.

2. With this interesting piece of information, include the source, something that will jog your memory when you go back to write. I find the title of the article to be helpful, perhaps the author's name, the year the article was published and possibly the page in the article that the information was found on (use paragraph numbers for web articles that do not have page numbers).

Careful reading is essential to not plagiarizing. It is also the key to being original. As long as you set up an excellent bank of notes for yourself, you will find that you are well prepared to write. When you do write, take charge of the data.

Do not let other people's prose or spin on the data overshadow your own unique perspective. Put all of your sources away. Take all of your print-outs and books and stow them somewhere where you will not be tempted to look at them while you are writing.

In this way, you will not be tempted to hide behind someone else's writing style or turn of phrase, but instead will challenge yourself to develop your own voice. Keep only your notes out. Wherever you use data or findings from your notes, add a parentheses and either the title and year published or the author's last name and the year published. Whatever you do, have faith in your own ability to express your own unique perspective. Answer your own questions, develop your own exploration of the topic.

Be original. In finding your own unique voice, you may read many, many articles and books. While it may seem that there is nothing new under the sun, this is not true. Every time you write, you are creating something new that did not exist before this very moment.

Please note that there are many excellent sources on MLA, APA and AMA citations and references. It is not my intention to duplicate any of these materials. In fact, you may as well go to the source when you study these referencing styles.

For APA, visit the American Psychological Association at http://www.apastyle.org/.

For MLA, visit the Modern Language Association at http://www.mla.org/.

For AMA citation guides, visit the AMA Manual of Style at http://www.amamanualofstyle.com/.

This is not a complete list of citation sources. There are others such as Bluebook and Chicago Manual of Style, but this is a case of "same song, different dance". All of these guides use the same/similar pieces of information about the source to give credit to the research, data, statistics, theories or findings of other authors. In all of these styles, the intent is the same, to give credit where credit is due.

Sometimes, if I am in a hurry, I gather all my information about my source together and then visit http://www.citationmachine.net/

OR

http://www.bibme.org/

OR

http://www.citefast.com/.

There really is no crime in using a citation helper if you need to. It's not really cheating to plug your information into a tool and ask that tool to help you to format that information correctly. You still have to do all the legwork. You still have to do all the research, come up with your presentation of those ideas and fact-check all your data. Consider citation helpers like using a GPS instead of a road map. You still have to determine your destination, and you still have to drive the car. If you end up somewhere you didn't plan to be, then, that is on you. You are the driver. The GPS is just a tool. If you remember that you are ultimately responsible for the results of your work, then use whatever tools help you to put out a quality product.

Frame the data

One frequent mistake that writers often make is a reliance on the data as if the numbers speak for themselves. A picture may speak a thousand words, but numbers do require words to help put their meaning or significance into perspective. For example, simply stating that the United States signed The Declaration of Independence in 1776 does not tell the reader what he or she is supposed to gain from this fact. Perhaps the writer wants to point out the long colonization relationship with Britain which existed for more than a century before this date. Perhaps the writer wants to highlight the two centuries since this time period in which the United States has been self-governing. Perhaps the year itself is of interest because of other events that were occurring around the same time. Data requires context in order to be meaningful. Do not make the mistake of thinking that the data can tell the whole story.

For this reason, I tell my students that data is like a beautiful painting that requires a frame. Data can no more be dropped into the middle of a piece than a guest speaker can be dropped into the middle of a presentation. Both require an introduction. There is some point or purpose in sharing this data, just as there would be a point or a purpose in bringing in a guest speaker. Find that purpose. Before you even include the data, ask yourself what it is that you hope this data will show, prove or shed light on.

When you do share your data with a proper citation of course (AMA, APA, MLA, etc.), do not make the mistake of thinking that the data will tell the story for you. Data can be seen from many different angles. This is like the story from India about the blindfolded men and the elephant. One felt the trunk and thought this was a snake. One felt the leg and thought this was a tree. Each saw the elephant from a particular angle and each was right. Data and research findings are a little like this. In order for the reader to make the connections that you hope that they will make, you need to analyze the data for them and show what the data means. How does this data illustrate your point? Why is this data important?

Suffice it to say that you need to draw some conclusions from the data. If the data is viewed in this particular light, what is the take-away lesson from this?

I like to use the following mnemonic for framing the data:

Point

Examples

Analysis

Point

You can remember this as **PEAP** if you like. This means, tell us the point you wish to make. Share with us the data, examples, statistics, facts, research, etc. that you believe help to support your point. Analyze why these examples are relevant, groundbreaking, definitive, or important to consider. Draw conclusions as to what the data shows. Sometimes, this simply requires returning to or restating the point that you began with.

Exemplia Grata:

Point: More autism research is necessary.

Examples: Give the data on how many children are diagnosed with autism each year.

Analysis: Is this number high or low? How does this number compare to previous years? How quickly is this problem escalating?

Point: If we do not know what is causing autism, then we need to make it a priority to find out. For this, we need more research dollars.

Can you see why a number out of context might not tell as much of the story as you would like it to? Can you see why numbers, like great guest speakers, need a proper introduction? What numbers or statistics have you encountered lately which could be interpreted in more than one way?

Trends versus opinions

Everyone has an opinion.

By now, you have probably guessed that if all you have to offer is your opinion, then you are probably only going to attract readers who share your opinion. My mother has an old saying, "so and so is just preaching to the choir." What that means is that if someone has committed the time and energy to sing in the choir, then they are probably already true believers. Whatever the minister says, if he is preaching to the choir, his message is not reaching anyone new.

This is the problem with opinions.

Therefore, you would want to be careful with expressing opinions, especially in your opening or introduction. Opinions can turn readers off instantaneously.

There is, however, a key difference between expressing an opinion and expressing a trend. And the difference in wording can be very subtle.

Let's take the following statement as an example.

Ex. G. Opinion

All welfare moms are high school dropouts.

Let's look at the problems with this statement. The first problem is the word "all" and the second problem is the word "are".

For a number of reasons, you would want to avoid wording that expresses absolutes such as all, none, always, never, and so on. Why? The reason is that these statements are basically impossible to support. Out there, somewhere, there is a welfare mom who made it through college. Out there, somewhere, there is probably an exception to the rule. If you want to trip yourself up before you even start, these generalizations will definitely do that for you. The argument will then turn to discussing the exceptions as opposed to discussing whatever it is that you wished to discuss.

You can, however, come at the same topic from the side without raising as much ire by presenting it as a trend. In this case, you need to replace the "all" and the "are" in the previous statement.

Ex. G. Trend

Many welfare moms may be high school dropouts.

You could have used a number of words here to quantify your statement. You could have replaced all with many, some, a few, etc. The key here is that instead of making an indefensible statement, you are discussing a trend. At that point, counter-arguments have to address whether or not this is a trend, rather than whether or not there is a single exception.

In a similar way, you need to replace "are" with any of the modal verbs which would include verbs like may/might, can be/could be or include some sort of quantifier such as potentially, possibly, on the whole, in general, etc.

Play with these quantifiers. When you feel the urge to write an opinion, ask yourself how you could restate that in order to discuss a "trend" as opposed to an opinion. Trends leave room for discussion. Opinions usually do not.

If there is one thing that you have learned on your writing journey, it is that the act of writing itself is one wherein you want to open up lines of communication, never shut them down.

The intricate relationships between openings and closings

Yes, I know how that title sounds, and I meant it to sound that way. Opening paragraphs are sometimes called introductions. Closing paragraphs are sometimes called conclusions. Yes, these two parts of any article, essay, or book have a complex relationship. At the very least, the opening shows what you as the writer hope to achieve in the paper. At minimum, the conclusion reflects upon what you have successfully explored in the paper. However, this is a very simplistic view on how openings and conclusions interact with one another.

Here are a number of other relationships that you may see between the two.

Q&A: The opening may raise questions. The conclusion may answer those questions.

Past&Future: The opening may show the background or history of the issue. The conclusion may show the trend or possible future for the issue.

General-Specific&Specific-General: The opening may move like a wide angle lens panning in from the big picture and set up the specific issue. The closing may use the same lens and pan out to show how this specific issue impacts the big picture.

Illustration Mirrors: The opening may set up a poignant illustration to draw the reader in. The closing may return to another similar illustration to complete the picture.

Definition&Applications/Permutations: The opening may define the topic that is being dealt with. The closing may reflect upon applications for the given topic or permutations relevant to the topic.

Shock-Analysis & Call to Action: The opening may start with a shocking statistic and explanation as to why this statistic should cause the readership concern. The closing may draw upon that data in a call for action.

There are many, many patterns in writing. The more you study other writers, the more patterns you will be able to recognize and identify. The patterns listed above are some of the more basic patterns. At best, introductions and conclusions mirror each other, but often, introductions and conclusions have a complex relationship which speaks across the paragraphs of the paper like a long distance relationship, like letters sent across an ocean, reflecting upon the same thoughts and ideas from different locations under the stars.

Have you ever struggled to write an introduction? Why do you think this was? Have you ever set your introduction and conclusion next to one another to determine how one was talking to the other?

Creating the illustration mirror

Illustrations are especially effective at bringing the reader right into the moment. If you are trying to make the reader really feel what it is like to be in a particular situation, especially one that might be foreign to the reader, then this may be the tool for you. The illustration mirror can bring far away places or invisible human plights to the reader's doorstep. Indeed, this tool often works best when the subject matter is something that knocks on the ethical and moral doors or pulls on the heart strings. I find that human interest stories often benefit most from this approach. Let's look at a potential example.

Topic: hunger in the inner city

In this case, telling us how many people are homeless or how much this problem costs society might not bring the reader into this discussion in a way that will make the reader want to take action. However, a picture is worth a thousand words, and thankfully, you do not need to create a thousand words to paint an effective picture. Moreover, your word picture can touch upon senses that a two-dimensional picture can only allude to.

First, you will need to brainstorm. In order to brainstorm effectively, you need to consider all your senses. Those senses are generally referred to as sight, sound, smell, touch and taste. However, as human beings, we have other ways to interpret experiences which are empathic. When we see someone in pain, we often tend to wince in response. We are also capable of deep thought, action, and reflection. The complete human experience is what we are going for. These unseen facets are what can make a word picture actually far superior to an actual picture.

Let's start brainstorming.

What would you see? Block after block of absentee landlord properties, sometimes with roof or window damage. Boarded up buildings. Small storefronts with bars on the windows. Children playing in the streets with someone as a lookout. Gangs of youth gathered at the corner.

What would you feel? A sense of emptiness, apprehension, hopelessness, and hunger.

What would you hear? City noises, cars moving over roughly paved streets, people shouting, a baby crying.

What would you smell? At dinnertime, an absence of cooking smells wafting into the street.

What would the physical sensation be? Hunger is like a burning pit in the stomach that is hard to ignore.

What would you do in this situation? It would seem easy to just go out and buy food, but for blocks and blocks, there are no grocery stores, only high-priced convenience stores which sell junk food at prices meant to offset the risk of doing business in the inner city. The only way to buy food would be to get on a cross-town bus and ferry as much food as a person can carry on his or her person through public transit.

What might you think? Continual hunger can make it tough to think about anything else. It can drive out of control behavior, anger, or deep resentment. When food is so expensive that it is out of reach and there is no way to get food, this can drive rising levels of crime.

Let's reflect upon this brainstorming exercise. First off, you probably learned that there is so much more that a word picture can do than an actual picture. There may be ways to portray some aspects of the scenario above in a photograph, but it would be a challenge to effectively portray all of this. This is why I think I would rather be a writer than a photographer. Since it is not a choice, it would actually be sublime to be passing good at both skills.

As you put it all together, you may choose to move senses around for heightened effect. Some descriptions may need to be expanded upon and others left out. This is where writing is an art form. After you have used your observational powers to brainstorm, you will want to spend some time crafting these observations into a passage that makes the reader feel as if he or she is standing there watching this scene as well.

EXAMPLE:

At dusk in the inner city, there are the smells of gasoline and garbage, but even when the wind picks up, even with open windows on an autumn evening, it is surprising how absent the smells of cooking food are. In such a densely populated area of run-down houses, some with broken windows or boarded up windows, crumbling pavement and pock-marked streets, it would seem that there should be food shops. Yet, blocks and blocks of housing shows nothing more than a few brave convenience store keepers with metal grills over the doors and windows. The food inside is outrageously expensive as vandalism and the threat of violence is high, and it's little wonder. Young children play on the streets and gangs of youth gather on the corners, but there is a sense that hunger is never far away, that it is a gnawing pit that keeps drawing the attention back to a need that cannot be filled. And there is not much that can be done? The only grocery stores are a cross-town bus ride away. The brave traveler can only bring back as much as he or she can carry in two hands. This is hardly enough, so it is little wonder that hunger drives anger, violence and even crime. It is a response to a situation that seems to be without hope.

Please note that the illustration model often creates a rather powerful emotional appeal. Be careful with this. Try to be as objective as you can about the picture and try not to go overboard with blame or hate wording. Your aim is to bring the reader into this picture, not serve the reader with a summons or a sermon. However, from here, your reader is probably hooked. He or she will probably trudge through an exploration of the elements that help to create and perpetuate this problem in the hopes that by doing so, analysis will shed light on possible solutions. This is where your conclusion can actually reflect back an answering image. It need not be the same image. In fact, it is best if the image sheds light on a different aspect of the picture or an answering picture.

For this, I would like to look at an inner-city, urban agriculture project which was created to answer the plight of urban hunger in Milwaukee, Wisconsin. As of this writing, Will Allen has created an inner-city greenhouse and growing project, Growing Power, on derelict city land that is producing low cost fruits, vegetables, eggs and fish for local families. Families can also join community supported agriculture and receive a portion of what is grown each week automatically and at a reduced cost.

What would you see? In the midst of an urban landscape, there are greenhouses and a farm store. Young people are working after school around the place, cleaning and ferrying produce. Inside the greenhouses is a tropical vision in which huge ponds of tilapia and trout are fed freshened water through beds of lettuce suspended above the tanks.

What would you smell? There are smells of ripe strawberries in vertical pots and ripe tomatoes.

What would you feel? Community spirit, a feeling of gratitude and abundance, a sense of what people can do when and where they work together.

What do you hear? There are people at the farmer's stand in front laughing and sharing recipes as they shop just a short walking distance from their houses. There is the sound of chickens clucking and youth workers gathering eggs for the market.

What would your physical sensation be? Trying out a taste of the produce, biting into a fresh strawberry or tomato, holding a heavy basket of foods to bring home and prepare for dinner, enjoying the feel of the sunshine.

What would you think, act or reflect upon this experience? This is something that brings out the best in people because it shows them how they can be empowered by working together for a common cause. This is a model that should be built in inner city areas where hunger is a real issue. The problem has a solution, low cost, high yield community gardens that bring the food to the people.

Where did I find all this information? The APA source for these observations would be Growing Power's nonprofit website, www.growing power.org, and Will Allen's book, The Good Food Revolution, which was published in 2012 by Gotham Books in New York City. An APA citation for this source might be (Allen, 2012). Considering that I am highlighting a specific solution, a citation would be warranted here in case the reader wished to study this solution and learn more.

Again, the artistry of brainstorming lies in bringing all the elements together in the most compelling way. Do remember that the prime real estate space in the conclusion is in the last few sentences. This is much like leaving a calling card with the reader because the last few sentences of the piece are the ones the reader is much more likely to remember word for word. Therefore, you do want to save the best for last.

EXAMPLE:

Urban hunger has taken a different path in Milwaukee, Wisconsin where Will Allen has created a nonprofit organization called Growing Power (Allen, 2012). Growing Power has taken derelict inner city land and turned it into a community garden project. The feeling itself is so much different from so many inner city landscapes. Here, youth volunteer in the greenhouses where fish laze about in the ponds, salad greens grow in beds above. Every inch of space is used. Chickens cluck and volunteers gather eggs. Meanwhile, out at the street, mothers and fathers take their time to talk, shop, and exchange recipes. The feeling is one of community and gratitude for what a community can do when all its members work together. Today, poring over the brightly colored fruits and vegetables, the feeling is also one of abundance and freedom from fear and worry. There are solutions to urban hunger. It takes a vision and energy, but not more energy than the pain and suffering of doing nothing.

Let's look at this answering paragraph. Put the introduction/opening and the conclusion/closing side by side. In this case, one illustration is presenting the problem and the other illustration is presenting the solution. These paragraphs complement each other and speak to one another. If you enjoyed the image created in the closing paragraph here, it was actually inspired by the work of Will Allen. You can find out more about his work at www.growingpower.org.

In your own reading, can you feel the relationship here between the opening and the closing? How have you started to take a closer look at openings and closings and their relationships in the articles that you have read this week?

Definition versus Application and Analysis

This pattern is one that I perfected more closely while working with Paul Preiss, Nicole Tedesco and Neil Halpern with the International Association of Software Architects and Microsoft. Definitions can be dry. Applications can seem pretty dry as well, but sometimes the compelling part of the article is the body of the piece in which the writer can tell a story. Sometimes, the piece is a success story. Sometimes, the piece is a cautionary tale. However, the impact of bringing these diverse elements together is that they can create a compelling, textured landscape within which to examine an issue.

Let's say that the topic is the user experience. For obvious reasons, as you start out upon this quest to explore this topic, you are going to have to define and explain what the user experience is. This is a situation of speaking lingo. If everything sounds like Thai to the reader, it does not matter how wonderfully it is executed, the reader will have no appreciation for it. Therefore, as we start out, we have to fill in some of the knowledge gaps that may impede a true conversation between the writer and the reader.

For definition paragraphs, I like to answer the W questions (and one H question). What is it? Who uses it? When and where would you use it? How is it created? Why is it important? Be careful with the why question as this one can lead into an entire dissertation--quite easily. In fact, any of these questions with enough analysis and reflection could turn into its own paper. However, in a definition paragraph, be mindful that the goal is just to bridge gaps in background knowledge. Truly understanding the nature of the beast is going to be the work of the body of the paper.

Brainstorming a definition for the User Experience:

What is it? The User Experience is the "real feel" experience that a computer user has when using a program. This can refer to how comfortable the program is to use or anticipate , how well the program meets the user's needs, and how satisfied the user is with the experience and results overall.

Who uses it? Designers and programmers work together to try to address these concerns as they create software.

When and where would you use it? If humans are going to be using the program, and there are some programs that are written for machines who may have fewer aesthetic concerns, then the program has to bear in mind the needs and the prior experiences/knowledge/skills of the general user.

How is it created? Sometimes, designers survey test audiences to find out their needs and may have live users try out the software to figure out where the human-induced errors and glitches are likely to happen.

Why is it important? Programs need to create a desirable human experience because this is the consumer. Consumers will buy programs that meet their needs, and will often not buy programs which do not.

This sort of brainstorming experiment often does not need an awful lot of artistic play in order to make it readable. Watch how this definition introduction comes together without the scaffolding.

DEFINITION INTRODUCTION EXAMPLE

The User Experience is the "real feel" experience that a computer user has when using a program. This can refer to how comfortable the program is to use or anticipate how well the program meets the user's needs, and how satisfied the user is with the experience and results overall. Designers and programmers work together to try to address these concerns as they create software. If humans are going to be using the program, and there are some programs that are written for machines who may have fewer aesthetic concerns, then the program has to bear in mind the needs and the prior experiences/knowledge/skills of the general user. Sometimes, designers survey test audiences to find out their needs and may have live users try out the software to figure out where the human-induced errors and glitches are likely to happen. Programs need to create a desirable human experience because this is the consumer. Consumers will buy programs that meet their needs, and in general, will not buy programs which do not.

In the IASA project, Nicole and I worked with authors to create a defining experience, a moment in which the issue, in this case of the user experience, was played out in a way that even a novice could feel and see. Narrative story has many powerful applications here as the writer can tell a story of how all the elements of the user experience come together to create a tale of success. On the other hand, a cautionary tale works just as well to show how forgetting or not dealing with one crucial piece early enough or well enough can impact the whole product experience. I will leave the story to your imagination.

The relationship of the introduction to the conclusion is what we are studying here. In this case, the most important question is why. Why would the programmer take steps to plan for the user's experience? Why would the designer be concerned with the user's hopes or expectations for the program? Why should the user experience be factored in early in the design cycle? Why does a failure to plan for the user experience often predict failure for the program on the open market? If the opening answers the easy questions and the body explores what this really means in terms of real world planning and development, then it is fair that the conclusion can focus on the more in-depth questions which are frequently how and why.

CONCLUSION: THE TAKE-AWAY LESSON (ANALYSIS)

The lessons regarding the user experience need to factor into the software design process. Indeed, sometimes users do not always know completely or can articulate well all the outcomes that they wish the program to create. Sometimes, the program can be well into the testing phase when it is realized that the user requires other functions or heightened capabilities from the program. This can impact the bottom line, push the development of the program past deadline and can affect the marketability of the program. Knowing what the user wants and expects is a primary piece to the development puzzle. Ignore it at your own peril.

In this conclusion, we are going to assume that the story was a cautionary tale. However, what I would like you to do right now is to put the introduction and the conclusion side by side. Do you see how these two pieces speak to one another? One opens the conversation. The other closes the conversation. The subject of the body and the creation of effective story writing is a subject for another chapter.

As you have been reading this week, have you encountered the definition-application/analysis pattern? Why do you think this pattern might be an effective teaching tool in the classroom or workplace? How can you make work-related jargon easier to understand?

The past touches upon the future

There is absolutely nothing wrong with a chronological approach. Chronological means governed by time. In fact, some of the most complex subjects really ought to be presented in some of the most simplistic pattern designs. I would not say that there is an inverse relationship between the complexity of the subject matter and the complexity of the presentation, but there could be. Imagine this. You are at a lecture with a researcher of mitochondrial disorders. This topic is pretty heavy although the subject matter itself is light. We are talking about cells and their metabolism of energy here. If the researcher just jumps in and starts talking about current research or worse, heaven forbid, a comparison of the various research models, 99% of his audience may nod off, drooling from brain processing overload. This is a situation where the chronological approach may work best for a lay audience.

This relationship between past and future is important. The past tells us what we already know, or think we know. The future tells us what we want to know or hope to learn. The logical progression is to move from some place in the past where we can explore what we have learned and how we know what we think we know to some place in the future and all of its possibilities. This is important.

Remember that when you are giving background knowledge, you are quickly bringing the readers up to speed. The primary question that you need to ask yourself in this case is what does the reader need to know in order to be able to understand the rest of the article? To do this, you need to think about what the average reader does know. Would the average reader understand the key terms. Is there some way to explain these terms without bogging down the piece?

Let's look at an introduction example covering the past and necessary background knowledge. The topic is hyperbaric oxygen therapy.

Brainstorming: What will the reader know already? What will the reader need to know?

What is hyperbaric oxygen therapy? What is the theory behind this? What is oxygen? Why is oxygen important to cellular healing? Where did this idea come from?

Let's look at a conclusion example covering the future, the potentials for future advancement and applications of hyperbaric oxygen therapy.

What are the take-away lessons here? What new developments are going to come out of this field? Why should this be exciting for the audience?

Sometimes, simple is elegant. Can you see how these two sections would talk to one another? The body paragraphs for this piece could be as wonderful and as complex as the research that is currently underway right now.

What complex subjects can you see benefiting from a simple presentation design? Why does your audience's background knowledge matter? Where might you use this pattern?

Comparing and Contrasting

If you have ever folded a piece of paper in half and written on one side all the pros to an argument and on the other side all the cons to an argument, then you know a little about comparison and contrast. When one compares two ideas, one is looking for the similarities between the two things. When one contrasts two ideas, one is looking for the differences. Ultimately, one is usually comparing or contrasting in order to figure out what the better choice is in a given situation.

Let's say that one is trying to explore whether cyberschooling or home schooling is the better choice for one's child. Of course, one can write out the pros and cons, but in the end, this really only helps the individual to make up his or her own mind. Let's say that this same person needs to convince his or her parents that this is the right choice for their grandchild. At the point that one has to present one's argument to other people, a lot more information needs to be formatted and presented.

Let's begin with this premise. Comparisons show similarities. Contrasts show differences. Meaningfully, however, you can only contrast two things which have some essential common ground. For example, it would be meaningless to contrast an orange and an automobile. What would be the point? However, if one were considering a diet, one might meaningfully contrast saccharine and nutrasweet. This contrast might be a meaningful discussion for someone who is purchasing diet foods. The key issue here is that saccharine and nutrasweet have some key factors in common. They are both artificial sweeteners. They are both low calorie, sugar substitutes. They both appeal to dieters as a means to lower their caloric intake. They are both man-made substances, which may present health concerns.

Before you can argue the differences between two things, it is important to figure out what these two things have in common. You need to set up that common ground first because usually the common ground is what gives meaning in the first place to the discussion. In the case of the parent who is trying to decide whether to home school or cyber-school, it is important to determine what these two things are and how they might be similar. You may wish to use a Venn diagram as you explore this concept. Try drawing two overlapping circles. Where the circles overlap, show all the qualities that these two items share. Where the circles are separate, show how these two concepts are different. This is a great way to brainstorm.

When one is writing the piece, one may wish to set up the common ground first. This does, in effect, explain why the comparison is actually meaningful. For example, if you were comparing cyber-schooling and home schooling, you might want to point out that both of these options are alternatives to regular, public school. Both require a motivated student who will study on his or her own from home. Both serve as options for children and families for whom the public school is not a good choice, for personal, medical or social reasons. Sometimes, parents choose alternatives to public school because they want to have more impact over their children's lives, and to spend more time together. Do you see how setting up the comparison, how these two things are similar, sets up the framework for discussing how these two things are different?

Usually, when one is comparing two ideas, one would want to choose some key factors to explore. In this case, you may wish to look at how home schooling and cyber-schooling differ in terms of the methods of teaching, how home schooling and cyber-schooling differ in terms of grading, and how home schooling and cyber-schooling differ in terms of curriculum. That these two ideas share these common factors makes it possible to contrast how these two approaches handle these factors differently.

For example, while both homeschoolers and cyber-schoolers have to meet certain local or state standards with regard to curriculum, they may do so differently. Homeschoolers may buy a curriculum with books and exercise workbooks on various topics. Homeschoolers may work through these studies on their own and at their own pace. Cyber-schoolers, on the other hand, buy into the curriculum which has been developed by an online school. There may not be as much freedom, but there may be more structure. Often, cyber-schools have less flexible schedules and deadlines for completing curriculum. The takeaway lesson here is that home schoolers who enjoy developing their own studies might feel boxed in by the format of the cyber-school. However, families who are uncertain of their ability to home school may appreciate that intermediate step from public schooling to cyber-schooling from home.

Do you see how this comparison/contrast is set up? You can only contrast what you can compare. In the end, you will want to consider your reader's reasons for reading this article. Is your reader in a position to make a choice? Is your reader considering the benefits and drawbacks of two different choices? In the end, is your reader using this article to help him or her to make a choice?

This is why you would want to close such a piece with an analysis of which choice might be the better choice. Better is such a subjective word. What is better for one person might not be better for another person. However, you, as the writer, might be able to distill the essence of the argument down for your readership. In the case of the home schooling/cyber-schooling topic, you might want to distill the discussion down to this essential question. Most families who make a decision to study from home have decided to step outside of the public school system. The decision to home school or to cyber-school seems to be based on confidence. Parents who are very confident in their ability to teach their own children may choose home schooling because there is more autonomy and because it may be cheaper. Parents who are less confident or who have less free time may choose to cyber-school since the curriculum and all learning activities are laid out. For some parents, the age of the child is a factor. It may be easier to teach children the basic skills in the lower grades, but even seasoned home schooling parents may choose to cyber-school in junior high and high school as the subject matter becomes more advanced.

Where do you use pros and cons to analyze choices in your life? How can a comparison/contrast approach help to explore those options, or present those options for others to consider?

General-Specific and Specific-General

This is precisely the type of pattern that you may want to use when you are working with a topic that is so specific that the reader may not have an easy time just jumping into it. Alternately, your topic could be an abstract concept that is so generalized that different people have a different definition of the word.

Imagine your introduction like a zoom lens. Your topic may be a picture that is so close-up that it is difficult to make out what the picture is supposed to represent—unless, of course, you are an expert. Imagine that you have a zoom lens and you can widen your focus and widen your focus again till you can effectively see the big picture.

Consider your topic.

Let's talk about concrete topics first. There are some topics that are easy to relate to like mint chocolate chip ice cream. You can almost see it in your mind. If you have ever had mint chocolate chip ice cream, you may even remember exactly what it tastes like. Even if you have never had chocolate chip ice cream, the name itself is descriptive enough for most people to imagine it. This is what is called a concrete topic. You can see it. You can touch it. You could even go buy some at the grocery store. This is not the sort of topic that requires a general-specific warm-up in order to engage the reader.

Some concrete topics are specific enough to require a general-specific treatment. Such a topic might be a place like Charlotte, North Carolina. This might require a little bit of a warm-up. You have to consider that some of your readers might never have visited this area, or may not be too good at geography. You may want a little bit of a warm-up. You may want to start with what they know, such as the US. Most people are familiar with the US as a country. Then, you may want to explore that the US has 50 states. Certain states are on the eastern seaboard. The eastern seaboard is traditionally divided into the north and the south. North Carolina is in the south, and Charlotte is a major metropolitan area that is almost directly in the heart of North Carolina and truly represents all the best qualities of a southern city such as beautiful weather, great community activities and southern hospitality.

Think about how we used that information to bring the reader up to speed. We even gave them a little bit of a preview as to what we want to talk about.

Abstract topics can similarly benefit from a general-specific treatment sometimes. Abstract topics are not so easy to get your hands on. Think about all the ideals that people lay down their lives for:

freedom, dignity, equality, love, success, and the pursuit of happiness. You may be able to come up with an image in your mind that relates to these topics. However, the image that you come up with may not be the same as the image that someone else comes up with. This is the true challenge of writing, knowing what you know about a topic and making accommodations for the fact that someone else may have an entirely different experience with that topic. In order to even address such a topic, you may need to establish some common ground.

Let's take a topic like "the pursuit of happiness". What does that even mean? To you, it may mean the ability to do things you like to do such as skiing or playing sports. To someone else, it may mean freedom from worry. To one person, it may mean having the support of a governmental social support network, and to another, it may mean just the opposite. Where did you first hear this phrase? Where do you think other people first heard this phrase? What prior knowledge would your reader have? What is the common ground here?

Most people have seen this phrase in association with Thomas Jefferson's penning of the United States Declaration of Independence. Among the things he stated citizens should have a right to would be "life, liberty, and the pursuit of happiness". Now, you might want to analyze how people define "pursuit" and how people define "happiness". Take apart the phrase. How do you think most people define the pursuit of happiness? Give some parameters for your definition. Concrete needs might be food, clothing and housing. We must assume that the pursuit of happiness is something well beyond this, an abstract concept that is not defined by something as simple as food, clothing, and housing. In your attempt to break down happiness, you may make a few enemies. This might be unavoidable. However, you may break down happiness into social and personal development goals. Rest assured, there is almost no way that you could define such a topic without offending someone. Handle with care. Do so as graciously as possible.

In both of these examples, you have taken your camera and moved from the big picture to a smaller subset of the big picture. You have done so because your reader might not have been thinking about this particular topic, or your reader may be outright unfamiliar with the topic. In either case, widening the angle on your lens so that you move from something that the reader is familiar with toward something that the reader may be less familiar with can be an effective way of starting your paper.

If the introduction has had your moving from a big picture and gradually narrowing your focus until you come to your specific topic, imagine what the closing will do.

It will do just the reverse, of course.

In the course of your paper, you may have explored very specific information about a particular topic, but all this information must be good for something, right? This is the question that the reader will probably be asking himself or herself as he or she comes to the end of the piece: "What am I supposed to get out of this?"

Take your camera and review the specific information and then zoom out a little at a time. Make the topic relevant to your reader.

If you were discussing all the qualities of Charlotte, North Carolina, you might want to start zooming out and discuss how this is relevant to your reader. Why might people considering a visit to the southern portion of the US want to consider visiting Charlotte, North Carolina.

In the same way, if you were writing about the social and personal aspects of the pursuit of happiness, you might want to begin to zoom out and explore why it is important to define what happiness is, even if it is only a personal definition. In short, return to the big picture and tell the reader why this topic is important or relevant.

What abstract ideas do you like to talk about in conversations with other people? How were you introduced to these ideas? Why do you think that your definition of this ideal or abstract concept might be different from someone else's?

Shock-Analysis and Call to Action

In writing, we sometimes talk about "hooks". The image that this is supposed to create is one in which the writer is a fisherman with a hook and bait; the readers are fish. Hooks can be anything which makes the reader want to keep reading. Sometimes, students mistakenly think that appealing to emotion or otherwise starting an argument will act as a hook. However, I find the best hooks are the kind that are irrefutable.

By this, I mean—give them the data.

For example, I could start with a generalization.

Ex. G. Blacks and minorities are overwhelmingly overrepresented among prison populations.

This is okay, but it leans very closely toward sounding like an opinion.

It might be better to use actual data to shock the reader to attention.

Ex. G.

As of 2013, Saki Knafo states in the Huffington Post's Black Voices Section that "One in every three black males born today can expect to go to prison at some point in their life, compared with one in every six Latino males, and one in every 17 white males, if current incarceration trends

continue"
(http://www.huffingtonpost.com/2013/10/04/racial-disparities-criminal-justice_n_4045144.html).

As a side note, using the website there in the parentheses instead of the author's last name and the year, or the name of the article and page number is what is commonly called "Cite Lite". It's not appropriate for collegiate or academic work, but you will frequently find it used in blogs and informal internet journals. If you are deciding whether to cite or not to cite, based on the amount of work involved, "Cite Lite" is preferable to not citing at all.

Also, Knafo's statement is a quote. This is why I put it in quotation marks. In general, it might be better to paraphrase if your paper is going to be evaluated by Turnitin, which is the evaluation system that most colleges and many high schools now use in order to catch plagiarism. In the case of Turnitin, it is simply looking for strings of words that appear elsewhere on the internet or in previously submitted papers. The system cannot identify whether or not you have properly cited your sources. Therefore, in order to maintain originality, it might be better to paraphrase.

Paraphrasing might look like this.

Ex. G. As of 2013, Sake Khafo states in the Huffington Posts' Black Voices section that up to a third of young black males may spend time in prison within their lifetime. That number is one in six for Latino males and one in 17 for white males. This is based on current rates of incarceration

(http://www.huffingtonpost.com/2013/10/04/racial-disparities-criminal-justice_n_4045144.html).

Since you are citing actual data, you still need to provide some form of a citation for your data so that your readers can actually go back and fact-check your information.

Now that we have discussed the elephant in the room, i. e. how to incorporate this data and give credit where credit is due, let's look at these numbers themselves.

How do you feel about these numbers?

How do you think your reader will feel about these numbers?

Do you think that the numbers are more compelling than just a generalized statement?

However, there is more to using a shocking statistic than just dropping it into the opening paragraph. Frequently, you need to explore or explain the nature of this data in the opening paragraph and explain why this data should be of concern to the reader.

For example, you might want to talk about the demographics of the US and explain that as of 2014, the US Census Bureau estimates that roughly 77% of the US population is white while Blacks comprise roughly 13% and Latinos represent roughly 17% of the population (http://quickfacts.census.gov/qfd/states/00000.html).

{Please note that I used "Cite Lite" again here. I am not advising this as a citation method, but I want to make sure that the Kindle version of this guidebook has clickable links.}

If one considers that Blacks represent a much lower percentage of the population and the highest percentage of the incarcerated population, questions inevitably arise as to why Blacks are so disproportionately represented.

This is where you can lead into your thesis statement and suggest that we may be dealing with social, educational or judicial inequalities or a combination of all three of these issues combined.

We have looked at how some shocking statistics can open up a piece and act as a hook.

However, you may be asking yourself how you would close such a piece. Think about it for a moment. If you have raised the specter of a problem that is so glaring that it demands a closer inspection, you may wish to close with a call to action.

A call to action basically urges people to take some sort of action, even if that action is simply that more research needs to be done. This is where you may want to consider the problem and pose potential solutions as you close this piece.

Types of Papers and Thesis Statements

This is the bane of college students everywhere. A professor might ask the class to write a narrative, an explication, a cause and effect paper, or a literary analysis. While this makes sense in theory, there are a few steps that any good student has to master in order to get his or her ducks in a row.

First off, you need to decide what you are writing about. Most professors will ask students to write a thesis statement. A thesis statement is actually helpful in terms of understanding what you plan to write about, what your angle is and how you intend to explore the topic.

I like to use this brainstorming tool:

Topic:

Attitude:

Parameters:

You can call this TAP for short. Let me show you how you can create a thesis statement for a few different papers.

Let's say that your professor has asked you to write a persuasive paper about gun laws in America. First off, "persuasive" means that your professor expects you to take a side and defend your position.

You might want to decide whether you are for or against gun laws. You can also choose some middle ground and explain your position. Remember that while your paper may defend your opinion, the entire paper cannot be opinions. You need to have some facts and some data to back up your opinion.

Here is a sample thesis breakdown:

Topic: Gun laws

Attitude: are essential in a civilized nation

Parameters: because guns can be dangerous in the hands of people who are not trained to use them, who are too young to understand the dangers that guns represent or who are not responsible for their own actions due to mental illness.

The parameters are often the most difficult to write. It's frequently easy to say what you are writing about and what you think about the topic, but explaining why is often difficult. Try to pick three reasons. I usually string these ideas together in three similar clauses which might all start with "that", "because", "who", etc.

In this case, I combined a "because" clause and a series of "who" clauses.

The finished thesis might look like this:

THESIS: Gun laws are essential in a civilized nation because guns can be dangerous in the hands of people who are not trained to use them, who are too young to understand the dangers that guns represent or who are not responsible for their own actions due to mental illness.

This little statement is a gem because it hides a lot more than you might realize. It hints that you might open and close with the idea of civilization and the things that we expect from living in a civilized country such as safety and the ability to travel freely without fear of violence—ideally.

It hints at the types of people who might not be eligible for a gun license. We might expect to see a paragraph on gun safety training and why this is essential. We might expect to see a paragraph on why children and young adults should not handle guns due to maturity issues. Lastly, we might expect to see a paragraph on why people who handle guns should practice good judgment. Therefore, we may wish to restrict gun ownership for people who are not mentally sound or stable. Your last paragraph might be a reflection on your opening.

You can see all of this in the thesis. It's an amazing little jewel, frequently tucked into the opening of your paper. This is why many people do labor over writing the thesis of the paper first.

However different thesis statements do come together differently.

For a persuasive paper, the thesis might be trying to give the reader reasons to believe as you do. In this case, the writer is trying to explain his or her middle ground. Hint: the middle ground is usually the most logical ground to defend as it represents a compromise between all or nothing extremes, which are frequently "pie in the sky" ideals anyway. For a persuasive paper, think about the reasons why we should feel as you do.

Narratives are essentially stories. Everyone loves a story, and unless, you are doing something fancy like starting "in medias res" or otherwise known as "in the middle of things" or including long flashback scenes, your typical story has an easy organizational pattern: past, present, future.

When people think about stories, they think about the movies that play in their heads. The first thing they think about is drama, action, "roll 'em". However, there are a lot of essays that benefit from a narrative touch. Any sociological change can be treated from a narrative point of view. You can talk about how we used to think about disabilities, how we approach disabilities today, and why technology may make the idea of disability a moot point in the future.

You can also approach most personal/soul searching topics from a narrative angle—even if you are not necessarily telling a story.

For example, if your professor asks you to write a paper about how your perceptions of college have changed since you started on day one, you could definitely use a narrative model:

Topic: My confidence levels

Attitude: have definitely improved since I started college

Parameters: because I started out unable to manage my time and I have since learned how to juggle many classes simultaneously.

THESIS: My confidence levels have definitely improved since I started college because I started out unable to manage my time and I have since learned how to juggle many classes simultaneously.

In this particular thesis, you may find yourself reflecting on being overwhelmed in your first few days of college. You may spend a paragraph or a few paragraphs telling the reader what this was like. Then, you may tell the reader about how you learned some strategies that helped you. You may spend a paragraph or several paragraphs talking about changes that you made. Lastly, you may spend a few paragraphs describing what good time management looks like and why it is important to your success.

Problems/Solutions and Causes/Effects

Thesis statements rarely come together as easily as I showed you in the previous section. Yes, I know. I made it look easy for your benefit, so you can see how it comes together when everything is working pretty well.

The problem is that writing is a journey of self-exploration. The more difficult topic may not necessarily be "What should I write about?", but rather "What do I think about this topic?"

If it is a topic that you have never considered before, go easy on yourself. Don't expect yourself to have all the answers when you start out. Some professors encourage free writing. I waver on this point. Free writing is an excellent tool except for when you have to go back and try to revise it and turn it into a finished draft. In that case, sorting out the meaningful from the random can be a crazy journey.

For that reason, I tend to ask writers to brainstorm instead. On a blank sheet of paper, I might ask them to tell me their topic and their attitude on the subject.

For example, if the student's topic is climate change and the student's attitude is that we need to do something about this problem yesterday, then that's the headline at the top of the page.

From there, I usually ask a group of students to give me ways that they could explore this topic. I like to see groups work together in this way because first off, great ideas often come out of the collaboration. Secondly, a group keeps these ideas in bulleted versions that are going to be easier to sort later.

Once you have a list of bulleted ideas, you have to sift and sort through your ideas to determine which are actually related to the topic. You will always have some left-field, random comments that probably distract from the main idea or would demand a paper of their own if, like Alice in Wonderland, you followed down that particular rabbit hole. Go through the list and determine the ideas that are relevant or irrelevant to begin with. I sometimes have students mark these as R or I. You can also just cross out the ones that you don't want to work with. That works too. I like to remind groups that are helping one student at a time that the writer is "king" in these discussions. While you as a team member may like a particular idea and may argue your case, if the "king" says no, then the answer is no.

EXAMPLE:

The oceans are a mess because of all that plastic.

We have to wean ourselves off of fossil fuels because they are producing too much carbon dioxide.

We need to look at solar or wind power.

Politicians need to stop denying the science.

We could use hydrogen power.

The ice caps are melting. We are seeing global flooding.

People are cutting down the rain forest.

We need a carbon tax credit.

Electric cars are way too expensive.

ANALYZING BRAINSTORMING:

While groups can come up with great ideas, groups also have to become pretty good at throwing some ideas away. First off, if your topic is climate change, then you have to be able to make the connection between each of these ideas and climate change. If it is too much of a stretch to keep it in the paper and the topic is definitely going to throw your world out of orbit, you may need to let it go for the time being.

For example, "The oceans are a mess because of all that plastic" may be relevant to pollution, but it may not correlate to the rising levels of carbon dioxide.

You may have to mark this one as "irrelevant" to the current discussion.

As a second example, "Electric cars are way too expensive" may have some connection to the topic as a reason why people are still driving gas-guzzling SUVs, but it may not be the main point you want to explore. You could tie it in by virtue of talking about how supply and demand affect the prices of products and why people need to demand electric cars. This is a cautionary tale. It could either work out well or really, really badly. You may want to set it to the side to see how the rest of your ideas come together.

REANALYZING BRAINSTORMING:

Once you set certain ideas to the side, you still do not have a paper outline because the ideas may go everywhere at once. You still need to find some logical pattern to your ideas.

Here is where I like to ask groups to play a game of either problem/solution or cause/effect. These two types of papers are very similar. Problems are frequently the causes. Solutions can be effects. A cause/effect paper is usually pretty objective. The paper may look at the causes and then look at the effects. There may not necessarily be a judgment value attached to this. A problem/solution paper is very similar, but with a different spin. After exploring all the problems, you may want to propose a solution.

In this case, let's have our group explore the problem/solution value of each of the following statements.

Climate Change is something we need to do something about....

PROBLEM AND SOLUTION We have to wean ourselves off of fossil fuels because they are producing too much carbon dioxide.

SOLUTION We need to look at solar or wind power.

PROBLEM Politicians need to stop denying the science.

SOLUTION We could use hydrogen power.

PROBLEM The ice caps are melting. We are seeing global flooding.

PROBLEM People are cutting down the rain forest.

SOLUTION We need a carbon tax credit.

ORGANIZING BRAINSTORMING:

Now that we have identified the nature of each of these statements, we can start to organize our ideas.

Logically, if you look at this from the reader's point of view, it is really impossible to get behind any solution unless he or she understands the problem first. Therefore, it doesn't make sense to lead with the solution. It makes sense to explore the problems first. Then, you can finish up with the solutions.

PROBLEMS:

Politicians need to stop denying climate change.

We are too dependent on fossil fuels and they produce carbon dioxide.

Carbon dioxide heats up the planet by trapping solar energy and not allowing it to escape. (This was added because as we looked at the problem, we realized we had left out critical information.)

In addition, we are seeing less carbon dioxide turned back into oxygen by trees because people are cutting down trees, especially the rain forest.

Rising temperatures are causing polar melting, rising ocean levels and natural disasters.

TRANSITION:

We can still do something about this if we stop denying the problem.

SOLUTIONS:

We need to stop burning fossil fuels for energy. We may need to implement a carbon tax.

We need to stop cutting down the rain forest. (This was added because we brought it up in the first part of the paper, so we have to address it here.)

We can develop renewable sources of energy such as solar, wind and hydrogen power.

FINDING YOUR THESIS AFTER BRAINSTORMING:

As you can see, sometimes, you may end up going through many stages of brainstorming before you figure out exactly how you feel about a topic. The brainstorming shown in the previous sections went through a few stages of development until it almost became a mini-outline. In fact, if you ask some key questions about each of those topics, I daresay that you may be able to launch right into writing your paper. The only thing that is left is to try to distill all this thinking down into a thesis statement.

Topic: Climate change

Attitude: needs to be addressed now

Parameters: by reducing our use of fossil fuels, by saving the rain forests, and by developing renewable energy.

THESIS: Climate change needs to be addressed now by reducing our use of fossil fuels, by saving the rain forests, and by developing renewable energy.

In the thesis statement, you hinted that you could be looking at both the problem and solution aspects of climate change. In fact, if you wrote this paper, you would do just that. Does this summarize everything that you might cover in the paper? No, of course, it doesn't. Still, it gives the reader a pretty good idea as to what your paper is going to be about, and that is the purpose of having a thesis statement.

Overview

Every night as Tadhg came home from working in the Writing Center at his college, he would recount the challenges of the day. I am a retired college professor, so these conversations could, as you can well imagine, go on for hours.

You might want to consider this book an icebreaker. It's the lead-in to a more interesting conversation about ideas, where ideas come from, how ideas change over time, how ideas change us, how ideas can effectively be presented to other people, etc. Writing is not just a physical act. It is not even a purely intellectual act. Writing is an act of synergy. When you are creating, you are firing on all cylinders, and that is a truly beautiful thing.

Some people call this "critical thinking". I kind of resent this term because people get caught up on the "critical" wording and forget about the "thinking" part of the equation. Let's just say that thinking happens on a number of levels from being blissfully unaware that other universes exist to being able to design the space ship and chart the maps that will take you there. In between this high and low point, there are a thousand shades of all the colors imaginable. This is what I like to call "creative thinking". It's even more fun when you "phone a friend".

Thus, it's our hope that after reading this compact little text about working with ideas that all your neurons will be fired up and ready for new explorations.

Go ahead. You can do it. Think creatively!

Commonly Misused Words

While I don't advise students to edit while they are writing since it really interferes with the creative process, when you are ready to edit, you may want to give a skeptical glance toward your spell-checker. Not all that we "right" is "write"—to give you one egregious example.

Many websites address the issue of commonly confused or misused words. These are some of the words that Tadhg and I have encountered in our work with students. However, for a more complete list of homophones, you can always visit

www.homophone.com.

Spell-checkers and grammar-checkers are somewhat rudimentary at present. Students often overestimate their capabilities. A spell-checker is only going to catch a misspelled word. Auto Correct may even exacerbate the problem by suggesting the wrong word for what you wanted to express. I once had spellchecker correct the word "amass" by suggesting "an ass". Imagine my horror if I had not edited that!

As always, be vigilant. If you aren't sure if you have the right word, there is no shame in looking it up in a dictionary. The following is a list of the most common offenders.

Ado/Adieu

Accept/Except

Affect/Effect

Aisle/Isle

Apart/ A part

Are/Our

Ascertain/Assert

Assess/Asses

Axis/Access

Ax/Ask

Bald, Balled, Bawled

Bazaar/bizarre

Bear/Bare

Beat/Beet

Buy/Bye/By

Calk/Cock

Chalk/Chock

Chow/Ciao

Chord/Cord

Click/Clique

Come/Comb

Dam/Damn

Definitely/Defiantly

Desert/Dessert

Disc/Disk

Due/Do

Dye/Die (Dyed in the wool)

Erratic/Erotic

Fair/Fare

Fete/Feat/Feet

For all intents and purposes

Gist not Jist

Guilt/Gilt

Great/ Grate Greatful/Grateful

Hair/Hare

Herd/Heard

In synch (not in sink)

Its, It's

Knew/New

Know/No

Lessen/Lesson

Lets, Let's

Lien/Lean

Load/Lode

Magnate/Magnet

Mail/Male

Maybe/ May be

Mean/Mien

Mind/Mine

Might/Mite

Midst/Mist

Moat/Mote

Moral/Morale

Moue/Moo

Moot/Mute

Non Sequitur

None/Nun

Patience/Patients

Pare/Pear/Pair

Pain/Pane

Past/Passed

Plain/Plane

Plays/Place

Peace/Piece

Peeled/Pealed

Per se (not per say)

Petty/Pity

Poor/Pure

Prey/Pray

Present/Prescient

Prerequisite

Prerogative

Principle/Principal

Prints/Prince

Peek/Peak/Pique

Perspective/Prospective

Prerogative

Peers/Pierce

Psych/Sick

Regardless (not irregardless)

Regime, Regimen

Right/Rite

Road/Rode/Rhode Island

Role/Roll

Queue/Cue

Segue

Scene/Seen

Scent/Sent

Site/Cite

Stair/Stare

Steal/Steel

Sum/Some

Sundae/Sunday

Tale/Tail

Tear/Tier

Too/Two/To

Traitor/Trader

Threw/Through

Thyme/Time

Use/Used to

Verses/Versus

Vain/Vane/Vein

Vice Versa/Visa

View/Vue

Waist/Waste

Wander/Wonder

Which/Witch

Wither/Whither

Weather/Whether

Who/Whom

Who's, Whose

Meet the Authors

In the evenings after a long day at the writing center, Tadhg would sit down to a cup of chai with me and chat about the day. By the way, if I could be a fictional character from any animated series, I would be Uncle Iroh from Avatar. I have a deep respect for tea. After a cup of tea, a round of watering the plants, we would discuss why writing is not just the process of putting words on a page. It is the process of thinking, of taking apart an issue, of examining an idea from all sides. More and more, young people need to be able to not just know facts, but be able to analyze, interpret and construct arguments from these facts. Let's not call it critical thinking. Let's call it creative thinking, or even constructive thinking.

This little guidebook may be one small step toward that larger discussion. May you sit down with friends and discuss the greater issues at play in the world. This too is essential to the writing process.

Cover design by Falcon Giraux

www.ingramcontent.com/pod-product-compliance
Lightning Source LLC
Chambersburg PA
CBHW020539290526
45786CB00002B/955